MONUMENT MAKER

Daniel Chester French and the Lincoln Memorial

Written by **Linda Booth Sweeney** • Illustrated by **Shawn Fields**

TILBURY HOUSE PUBLISHERS
in association with the Concord Museum

History shapes our lives. And what we do with our lives can shape history. That's how it was with Daniel Chester French.

3

This is Daniel. He was born on April 20, 1850.

He was a sculptor. A sculptor uses clay, stone, bronze, and other materials to create statues and other works of art.

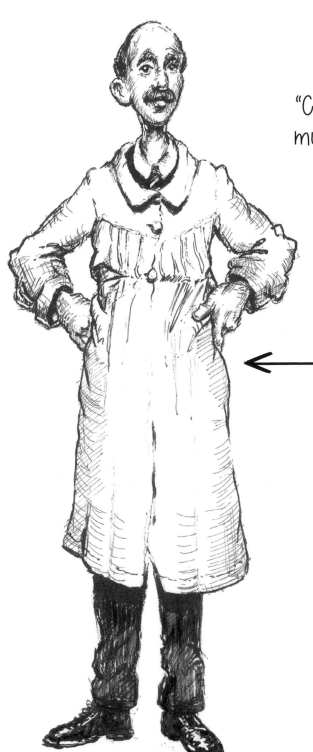

"Call me Dan. That's what my family and friends call me."

"Like my smock? It ← keeps my clothes clean when I work with wet clay."

There were very few sculptors in America when Dan was growing up. Becoming one was a bold choice, especially for a boy surrounded by successful lawyers and judges.

This is his story.

From the time he was a little boy, Dan liked to make things beautiful.

He lived on a farm in New Hampshire until he was ten, in a house built by his father. When Dan wasn't helping with the farm he was off exploring in the fields.

He decorated notebooks with names and drawings of the birds he saw: golden plovers in the marshes; bluejays and woodcocks in the woods; goldenwings and quails in the fields.

In 1860, Dan's father opened a law office in Boston, Massachusetts. The family moved to the busy town of Cambridge, renting a modern house with gas heating and an indoor bathroom. The poet Henry Wadsworth Longfellow lived down the street.

Talk at the dinner table was always lively. Sometimes the conversations were about the gate that needed fixing or the birds Dan saw that day. Sometimes the conversations were about more troubling things like the growing divide between the Northern and Southern states.

Abraham Lincoln was elected America's sixteenth president in the fall of 1860. The country was breaking in two over the issue of slavery. Before the end of the year, South Carolina became the first Southern state to split off from the Union.

In a speech on his first day in office, Lincoln said to the people of the South, "We are not enemies but friends." His calls for unity did not work. Ten more Southern states joined South Carolina to form the Confederate States of America, and on April 20, 1861, Robert E. Lee took command of the Confederate troops to lead them against the Union Army. The Civil War was beginning. It was Dan's eleventh birthday.

As the war dragged on, the family talked more and more often of friends and neighbors who were wounded or had died.

Dan did his best in school, though he often wished he was outside, tramping the fields with his friends.

There were birds to watch and beautiful things to make, like the snow lion Dan made with his older brother Will. It looked so real, some neighbors crossed the street to avoid it.

Soon after, Will left home to join the U.S. Revenue Cutter Service, which was trying to protect Union merchant ships from Confederate attacks.

On April 14, 1865, just before Dan's fifteenth birthday, the family heard awful news. President Abraham Lincoln had been assassinated. The great man who had led the country through the terrible war to a longed-for peace had been shot.

A few days earlier, the people of Cambridge had been celebrating General Lee's surrender in Virginia, which meant the war would soon end. Now they cried in the streets.

Girls and boys in Dan's school wore black bands on the sleeves of their dresses and shirts in the days that followed. Some people wore black clothes of mourning for months.

Dan would always remember Lincoln as the "man who saw straight when all the rest were seeing crooked."

Later that year, the family moved to western Massachusetts.
Missing his friends, Dan spent many winter nights lost in books
of Greek myths. In his free time, he drew gods and goddesses
on the plastered walls of the old shed behind his house.

In 1867 the family moved to the little town of Concord, Massachusetts, close to Boston by train. Dan's father said that the people of Concord were finer than the clothes they wore and the houses they lived in.

Concord Thinkers

Amos Bronson Alcott, 1799–1888
"Solitude is wisdom's school."

Ralph Waldo Emerson, 1803–82
"Insist on yourself. Never imitate."

Margaret Fuller, 1810–50
"Very early, I knew that the only object in life was to grow."

Henry David Thoreau, 1817–62
"Heaven is under our feet as well as over our heads."

Louisa May Alcott, 1832–88
"I am not afraid of storms, for I am learning how to sail my ship."

Nathaniel Hawthorne, 1804–64
"A single dream is more powerful than a thousand realities."

15

Dan loved his new town and its meandering river. When he wasn't canoeing, he worked on the family farm. He tended the cows, mended fences, harvested asparagus, and managed his own strawberry fields. Everyone knew when Dan had plowed the fields, because his furrows were the straightest and neatest.

Dan wasn't interested in studies, though. His grandfathers had been lawyers, and his father was a judge, but the law wasn't for him. He tried college but failed algebra, geometry, and physics. He returned to work on the farm, wondering what to do with his life.

What seemed like an ending
was really a beginning.

One spring morning Dan was in the barn bundling tender
asparagus to sell at the market when he spotted an
odd-looking turnip on the dusty floor. He started
to throw it into a bin, then stopped. The turnip's
split root and bulging white belly
reminded him of something.
He took out his pocketknife
and began to carve.

When he heard his sister Sallie calling him for lunch,
he was surprised. Where had the morning gone?

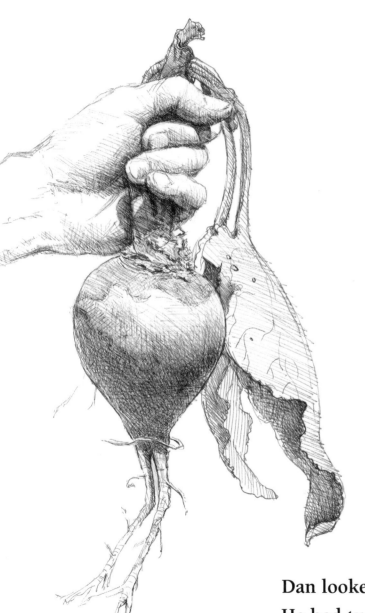

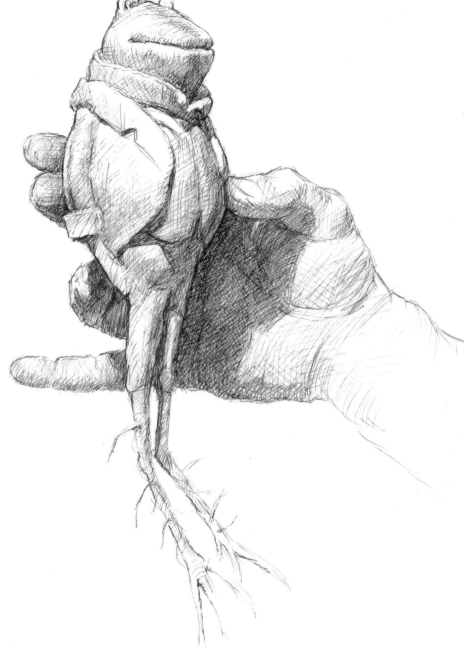

Dan looked at the turnip again.
He had turned it into a fine-looking frog!

But what good was a turnip frog? Dan tossed it on the kitchen table and went upstairs to wash his hands for the noon meal.

Gasps and laughter floated up through the old hallway floor. Halfway down the stairs, Dan heard his father say, "This looks like real talent!"

His stepmother whispered, "Well, what are we going to do about it?"

Dan learned something new that day: A turnip can turn into a frog. What might the son of a judge turn into?

Soon afterward, Dan's father returned from Boston carrying a cardboard box. In it was ten pounds of cold, wet clay for a family sculpting night.

One by one the family gave up, but not Dan. He kept at it until the shape of a dog's head appeared in his hands. From then on, Dan worked on the farm during the day and sculpted birds and animals at night.

Dan's neighbor May Alcott, sister of Louisa May Alcott, was impressed with his work. May was ten years older than Dan and a well-known artist. When Dan said he wanted to make a bust of his brother Will, May taught him how to build a wood-and-wire skeleton called an armature so the head would not fall down. His fingers worked easily, just as they did when he mended wire on the chicken coop.

Dan called this 1871 owl figurine Matchmaking.

May insisted that a sculptor had to learn to draw. Dan had never been interested in school, but now he wanted to train his eyes and hands.

For a while he attended the drawing classes May held in her barn three mornings a week. Then he took the train to Boston to study drawing and anatomy with a doctor who was also a sculptor.

He apprenticed for a month to a famous sculptor in New York City, where he learned by copying other sculptors' work. Once he spent three days copying a cast of a foot, and the details were still not finished.

Copying was a good way to learn. But could he create his own masterpiece?

When Dan was twenty, the people of Concord began planning for the hundredth anniversary of a famous battle fought right in their backyards. On an April morning in 1775, militiamen had rushed to the Old North Bridge to fight British soldiers from a garrison in Boston. Minutemen, as the militia were called, were farmers ready to drop their plow handles and grab a musket in a minute. It was the opening firefight of the American Revolution. In the words of Ralph Waldo Emerson, it was "the shot heard round the world."

The townspeople wanted a statue to honor the battle, and Dan wanted to make it. Other military monuments depicted famous generals, but Dan wanted to sculpt an unnamed hero, a man who could represent any of the local farmers who fought in the Revolutionary War.

Working night after night, he made dozens of small clay models on a table in his bedroom. At last he settled on four, each about the size of his hand.

After supper one evening, Dan carried the models into the parlor. At first his family all talked at once. Finally, they agreed on their favorite, a Minuteman leaving his plow and stepping forward with musket in hand. That was Dan's favorite too.

The hour was late. Dan wrapped the small statue in a soft cloth and ran to the home of his neighbor Ralph Waldo Emerson, the famous "Sage of Concord." Emerson and other committee members were meeting that night to discuss the monument. The committee liked Dan's model. With Emerson nodding agreement, they decided to give the young, largely self-taught sculptor a chance.

Three years later, on April 19, 1875, thousands of people crowded onto the Old North Bridge for the unveiling of Dan's statue. A biting north wind failed to chill the festive occasion. Judge French and his family led the procession. President Ulysses S. Grant came with the Marine Band from Washington, DC. May Alcott and her family were there. So were Henry Wadsworth Longfellow and Ralph Waldo Emerson. But one person was missing—Dan. He had already sailed by steamship to Florence, Italy, to study and work in the studio of Boston-born sculptor Thomas Ball.

31

Praise for the Minuteman statue rolled in. Dan knew he'd found what he wanted to do.

Just as Lincoln had hoped, America continued to change and grow in the years that followed. Dan did too. After two years in Italy, he returned to America. Messages from across the country arrived by mail, telegraph, and, later, by telephone, asking him to create sculptures for buildings, parks, cemeteries, and public places. Architects, city planners, and philanthropists commissioned him to create statues of monumental Americans who had helped shape the country.

Years passed. Dan became a husband, a father, a leader in his field, and a teacher. He became Daniel Chester French, famous sculptor. In 1915, when he was sixty-five, his friend Henry Bacon, an architect, made him his most monumental offer yet. Congress had put aside nearly three hundred thousand dollars for land, a building, and a statue in Washington, DC to honor Abraham Lincoln, and Bacon had been chosen to design the memorial. He wanted Daniel to sculpt a statue of Lincoln as the memorial's centerpiece.

So many statues of Lincoln had already been made. Daniel himself had created a standing Lincoln monument for the town of Lincoln, Nebraska. But the committee wanted this memorial to be something more.

The land for the Lincoln Memorial was swampy then.
The Potomac River bordered it to the west.

They wanted to bring the country together. Northerners and Southerners had fought side by side in the Spanish American War in 1898.

The committee wanted Daniel to create a fresh view of the monumental American who reunited the nation and ended slavery. Could he do it?

To the east, across what is now the National Mall, stood the US Capitol.

"It must be the most perfect statue of the man that human hands can design," Henry said. "It must seem to have a soul."

To find out, Daniel did what he always did—he did research. He read books and articles about Lincoln. He talked with Robert Todd Lincoln, the president's son. He studied casts that had been made of the living Lincoln's hands.

He pored over photographs of the great man's wise, craggy face. And he called on his boyhood memories of Lincoln, undimmed after all the years.

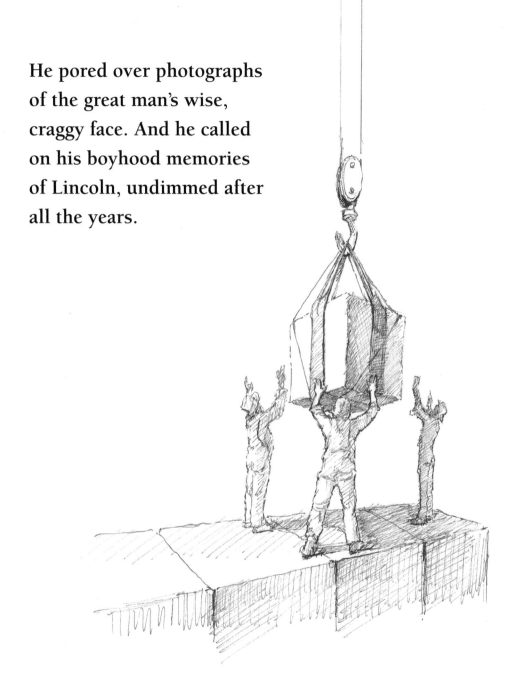

Meanwhile, the great memorial that would house Daniel's statue took shape.

Just as America was built by many hands, so was the Lincoln Memorial.

Blocks of white marble for Daniel's statue were blasted and cut from a Georgia mountainside by the sons and grandsons of American slaves.

The floor of the memorial was built of pink Tennessee marble, and the exterior was covered with marble from Colorado.

The steps were made of Massachusetts granite.

As he had done with the Minuteman statue forty years before, Daniel put on his smock and began to sculpt. In his quiet studio in the Berkshire hills of Western Massachusetts, he made 10-inch clay "sketch" models in different poses. He enlarged his favorite into a 3-foot-high "working" model, then began to sculpt a 7-foot- high model, shaping the large frame, bony face, long legs, and rumpled clothes of the log-splitter and country lawyer from Illinois.

In the spring of 1917, America entered the great war raging in Europe, and Southerners and Northerners once again fought shoulder to shoulder.

Ten-inch clay model.

Working model.

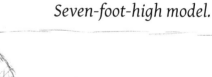

Seven-foot-high model.

Daniel

40

When the war ended, Daniel sent a plaster cast of his 7-foot clay sculpture to the Bronx, New York, studio of the six Piccirilli brothers, sons of Italian immigrants. The brothers had worked with Daniel for thirty years. No one was better at carving his sculptures into stone.

Attilio

Ferrucio

Furio

Getulio

Masaniello

Orazio

41

The Piccirilli brothers used a device called a pointing machine to enlarge Daniel's 7-foot plaster Lincoln into a 19-foot-tall stone version. It was hard and exacting work.

42

A single block of stone would have been too heavy to move, so the Piccirillis carved the statue in twenty-eight pieces. The blocks of marble were transported separately to Washington, then assembled in the memorial like a three-dimensional puzzle.

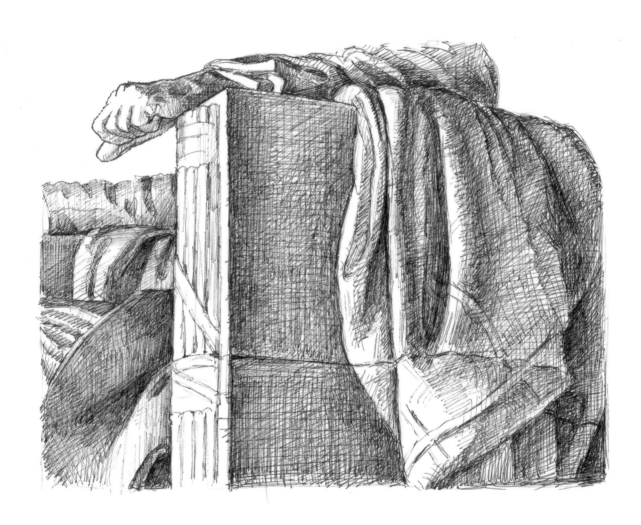

Daniel shaped Lincoln's hands with extra care.

One is balled into a fist to project the firmness needed to hold the country together. The other is open, as Lincoln needed to be, to hear the American people's many voices and move his country toward healing.

On May 22, 1922, seven years after Daniel
accepted the commission, the Lincoln Memorial opened.

Since then, untold millions of Americans have gone there to honor a great leader and the ideals he lived and died for.

Marian Anderson, 1939.

Martin Luther King, Jr., 1963.

Barack Obama, 2009.

They are the ideals—truth, justice, equality, charity, and unity—that bind America together . . .

. . . and that Americans are still striving for today.

When we need to be reminded of America's potential, the Lincoln Memorial and Dan's statue are there to inspire us.

Dan seeing his completed statue for the first time in 1922.

By shaping clay, Daniel Chester French helped to shape history. He sculpted more than a hundred monuments in his lifetime. His tribute to the tall, gaunt, noble man who held America together when no one else could have was the crowning achievement of a boy who loved to make beautiful things.

A Daniel Chester French Timeline

1850: Daniel French is born April 20 in Exeter, New Hampshire, to Henry Flagg French and Anne Richardson French. He has three older siblings—Henriette, William, and Sarah. (Daniel will later add a middle name, Chester, after the New Hampshire town where his grandfather lived.)

1856: Dan's mother, Anne, dies after a long illness. Dan spends a lot of time outdoors and is especially fascinated by birds. "I was an ornithologist before I became a sculptor," he will later write.[1] This boyhood passion will one day help Dan create spectacularly realistic wings on the angels he sculpts.

A drawing by Dan, age six.

1859: Henry Flagg French marries Pamela Prentiss, who becomes a second mother to Dan.

1860: The family moves to Cambridge, Massachusetts. Dan's father opens a legal practice in Boston. Dan meets William Brewster, who will become a famous ornithologist and lifelong friend; the two boys love to track birds and draw pictures of eggs, nests, and wings.

1864–66: Always eager to improve farming practices, Henry Flagg French becomes the first president of the newly formed Massachusetts Agricultural College in Amherst, Massachusetts (now the University of Massachusetts at Amherst). The family moves to Amherst in 1865, but the school is unable to embrace Henry's forward-thinking ideas. He resigns the position in the fall of 1866.

1867: Henry returns to his legal practice in Boston and moves with his family to a small farm in Concord, Massachusetts. Dan enters the Massachusetts Institute of Technology at his father's urging, living at home and commuting to MIT by train. He fails his classes there and resumes work on the Concord farm the following spring. His father writes:

> Dan works on the farm, taking a few hours off for sculpture when he pleases. I have given him the half acre of strawberries, which is now in full bloom, and I hope he will make from $100 to $200 out of it. He is a very good farmer and will know how to have his place in order when he gets one, if he does not follow farming as a business.[2]

1869–70: Dan creates a series of portraits of his sisters. The 18-inch-wide plaster portraits are sculpted in relief, with the image raised above a flat surface like a coin. He studies in New York with well-known sculptor John Quincy Adams Ward and takes anatomical drawing classes from Boston-based artist William Rimmer, drawing human and animal figures.

[1]Letter to Senator W. Murray Crane, January 30, 1907, Daniel Chester French Family Correspondence,, Library of Congress.

[2]Letter from Henry Flagg French to Benjamin Brown French, June 10, 1869, Daniel Chester French Family Correspondence, Library of Congress.

1870: Public statues are a way to tell a nation's stories. Dan is chosen to tell the story of the farmers who fought in the Revolutionary War. He later writes:

> When I was twenty years old, the town of Concord decided that a memorial of some sort should commemorate the famous Revolutionary battle…. My admiring friends ignorantly thought I could attack a job of any magnitude; and I was encouraged to go ahead.[3]

No payment is offered for the Minuteman statue, but it is a great honor to be chosen, and he accepts the commission. He immediately gets cold feet, telling his brother, "Of course, I have never made a statue. I wonder if I can do it?" His father reassures him, saying, "If that committee had the good sense to choose you, you must have the good sense to accept their invitation."[4]

Dan's 1871 figurine of an owl couple, Matchmaking *(see page 23) was cast in porcelain in England.*

1874: Dan completes *The Minuteman.* In October he sails to Florence, Italy, where, with financial help from his supportive family, he begins a two-year apprenticeship under expatriate American-born sculptor Thomas Ball. From the steamship *Atlas,* Dan writes:

> It makes me tremble sometimes, when I think of the things that my friends expect of me (or say they expect of me) for I am by no means sure that I shall ever accomplish anything higher than the ordinary. I shall try and do as much as in me lies, and hope as much for my friends' sakes as my own that I may not utterly fail.[5]

1875: The bronze Minuteman statue, draped in an American flag, is unveiled and dedicated on the bitter cold morning of April 19. It is the one-hundredth anniversary of "the shot heard round the world." Close to 30,000 people are in attendance.[6] The *Belvedere Standard,* a Chicago newspaper, calls it "one of the finest statues in the country."

When Dan completed his 7-foot-tall plaster Minuteman statue, it was cast in bronze by a foundry.

1876: While Dan works at his craft in Italy, his friend Ralph Waldo Emerson urges the town of Concord to pay Dan $1,000 for *The Minuteman,* saying, "If I ask an artist to make me a silver bowl and he gives me one of gold I can not refuse to pay him for it if I accept it." Dan's proud father reports Emerson's appeal in a letter to Dan.[7] Later that year, Dan returns from Italy and launches his sculpting career, settling first in Washington, DC and then back in Concord, where he builds a studio in 1879.

1884: In April, after the unveiling of his bronze statue of John Harvard in Cambridge, Massachusetts, Daniel receives a surprise letter of congratulations from the poet Emily Dickinson. She writes, "We learn with delight of the recent acquisition to fame and hasten to congratulate you on an honor so reverently won."[8]

1886: Having considered himself largely self-taught, Dan has long wanted more formal training in the art and techniques of sculpture. Now he travels to Europe to study drawing and modeling in Paris. There he immerses himself in the Beaux-Arts style of sculpture and architecture, which is named after the French national

---

[3]Tittle, Walter, "A Sculptor of the Spirit: How Daniel Chester French Puts Character into Marble," *London World To-Day,* 56 (December 1928), p. 201, cited in Richman, Michael, *Daniel Chester French: An American Sculptor* (1976).

[4] Cresson, Margaret French, *Journey into Fame* (1947).

[5] Letter to Henry Flagg French, October 29, 1874, Daniel Chester French Family Correspondence, Library of Congress.

---

[6] Holzer, Harold, *Monument Man* (2019), page 51.

[7] Letter from Henry Flagg French to Daniel Chester French, March 5, 1876, Daniel Chester French Family Correspondence, Library of Congress.

[8]Cresson, Margaret French, *Journey into Fame* (1947).

school of architecture. The opulent details and ornamental designs of this style are a favorite of America's industrial barons.

1888: Returning from Europe, Dan, now thirty-eight, marries his first cousin Mary Adams French and opens a studio in the back of their townhouse at 125 West 11th Street in New York City. This same year, the Piccirilli family of stonecutters (including the father and six sons) moves from Italy to New York and establishes a studio that will eventually fill an entire city block in the Bronx. Daniel will work with the Piccirillis many times to carve his plaster models into stone.

1889: Daniel and Mary's only child, Margaret, is born. Margaret will grow up to become an accomplished sculptor. Daniel finishes a bronze statue of Thomas Gallaudet, founder of Gallaudet University in Washington, DC, America's first school for the deaf.

1892: Daniel creates a bronze statue of Thomas Starr King, a minister and abolitionist who, during the American Civil War, worked tirelessly to encourage California to remain a part of the United States. (Abraham Lincoln credited King with preventing California from leaving the Union.) Daniel's statue of Reverend King now stands in Golden Gate Park, San Francisco, California.

1893: Daniel is asked by famed sculptor Augustus Saint-Gaudens to create six works for the World's Columbian Exposition—the World's Fair—in Chicago. One of them, *The Republic,* is a 65-foot-tall plaster statue of a woman covered in gold leaf and wearing a crown of electric lights. Welcoming the fair's 27.5 million visitors to the court of honor, she is nicknamed "Big Mary" by fairgoers. The second tallest statue in America in 1893 (at 305 feet, the Statue of Liberty is the tallest), Big Mary is destroyed by fire after the fair, but a 24-foot bronze replica is erected in 1918 in Jackson Park, Chicago.

1896: Daniel purchases Chesterwood, an old farmstead in the Berkshire hills of Western Massachusetts. There, with the help

The Republic, *Daniel's 65-foot statue for the Chicago World's Fair.*

of friend and architect Henry Bacon, he builds a studio and home where he will spend summers for the rest of his life. Daniel will write to his friend Newton Mackintosh in 1911, "It is as beautiful as Fairyland here now. The hemlocks are decorating themselves with their light green tassels and the laurel is beginning to blossom and the peonies are a glory in the garden. I go about in an ecstasy of delight over the loveliness of things."[9] He will create numerous sculptures there over the next thirty-five years.

1897–1914: Daniel's reputation grows as America continues to erect monuments to heroes in town squares across the country. Among his notable sculptures is a 9-foot-tall bronze statue (1910) of James Edward Oglethorpe, the soldier, founder, and governor of Georgia, who stood against slavery. The statue faces south so that Oglethorpe can

The Chesterwood studio with shades drawn on the many windows. Daniel's 10-inch clay model of the seated Lincoln is at right. At left is his plaster model of The Benediction, *which was cast in bronze in 1922 and is now in the collection of the Amon Carter Museum of American Art in Fort Worth, Texas.*

[9]Letter to Newton Mackintosh, June 13, 1911, Daniel Chester French Family Correspondence, Library of Congress.

"keep a watchful eye on the Spanish." In 1914, Daniel finishes an 8-foot bronze statue (on a 12-foot base by Henry Bacon) of Wendell Phillips to be placed in the Boston Public Gardens. Phillips had been a lawyer and speaker who, after hearing William Lloyd Garrison deliver an anti-slavery speech, became an abolitionist and spoke for the rights of African-Americans, Native Americans, women, and prisoners. Daniel wrote that he wanted to honor the man who "stood out against slavery in a manner to merit the admiration of anyone who loves a hero…. I should like it to represent what he stood for in the zenith of his power and usefulness…. At any rate, I am going to make my anti-slavery hero as inspiring as I know how."[10]

Daniel Chester French in 1915.

1915: Daniel is formally offered the job as the sculptor of the statue of Abraham Lincoln for the Lincoln Memorial. He will once again be working with Henry Bacon in what will be their biggest and most celebrated collaboration.

1922: Seven years after Daniel began working on his statue of the seated Lincoln, the Lincoln Memorial is officially dedicated on a warm, sunny Memorial Day. "I have lived with Lincoln so long that I feel as if he were a personal friend," Daniel writes.[11]

1931: Daniel continues to sculpt almost until his death on October 7 in Chesterwood, his beloved Berkshire studio home, at the age of 81. He had once told his daughter, Margaret, that if he had his wish, "I'd like to live to be two-thousand years old and just 'sculp' all the time."[12] His funeral is held at Chesterwood, and he is buried in Sleepy Hollow Cemetery in his boyhood town of Concord. Margaret designs a simple gravestone. Visitors to his grave often leave pennies, back side up, in memory of his seated Lincoln statue.

Daniel Chester French and Henry Bacon at the Lincoln Memorial in 1922.

"Look for beauty, not ugliness. Look for goodness, not evil. Look for cheer, not trouble."
—Daniel Chester French[13]

The Lincoln Memorial appeared on the back of the penny starting in 1959, the one-hundred-fiftieth anniversary of Lincoln's birth.

[10]Letter to Thomas Allen, November 9, 1912, Daniel Chester French Family Correspondence, Library of Congress.

[11] Letter to Katrina Trask, December 1,1918. Daniel Chester French Family Correspondence, Library of Congress.

[12]Cresson, Margaret French, *Journey into Fame* (1947).

[13]Letter with enclosure to Henry Corlerre, January 24, 1923, Daniel Chester French Family Correspondence, Library of Congress.

Author's Note

"There is nothing like being an artist, be it in paint or music or only mud."
—Daniel Chester French[14]

I've always been inspired by artists, those people who can use their imagination to create something new. My first art teacher was my mother. One day while her four rambunctious kids were at school, she put a sheet of plywood over an old ping pong table, and *voila!* an art studio sprang up in our basement. It wasn't fancy, but it became her place to create. I loved sitting at her elbow, turning found pine cones into wreaths, poking tiny holes into watercolor paper to make magical lampshades, and painting scenes from far-off lands on old boxes. I remember the steady stream of ladies who would show up with a crumb cake, then disappear into the basement. They were woodworkers, knitters, bakers, painters, quilters, and jewelry makers. Some of them became artists like my mother, but most of them simply enjoyed creating in the company of friends.

That artist's spirit is likely why, as an adult, I found myself living with my young family in a sculptor's studio that had been converted into a home. I hadn't heard about the artist—Daniel Chester French—but there was certainly a buzz about him in our newly adopted town of Concord, Massachusetts. I soon found out that he was a local hero, ranking up there with the Alcotts, Ralph Waldo Emerson, Henry David Thoreau, and other famous Concordians. The previous owners of the home had left behind photos of the studio during French's time. I imagined his models

Daniel in his Chesterwood studio, sculpting the model for the statue of George Washington in Paris.

sitting in the alcove where, a century later, my dog liked to poke his nose over the windowsill, waiting for my three children to get off the bus. I could imagine Dan in his artist's smock, hands filled with clay, buoyed by creative spirit, much like my mother and her friends.

As I got to know him, I began to see beyond the proper- and tidy-looking sculptor in photographs to the clever, largely self-made artist who broke from family tradition to follow his heart and eyes and hands. Eventually I convinced my family to follow the Daniel Chester French trail: We created a map of the many French statues in the Boston area and visited every one of them. Then we went farther afield, visiting the Lincoln Memorial and Daniel's other statues in Washington, DC. I pored through Daniel's letters and family papers in the Library of Congress. I stood quietly in front of his standing Lincoln statue in Nebraska, and the whole family stood in awe in front of his majestic statue of George Washington in Paris, France.

Daniel at Chesterwood with his 10-inch clay Lincoln and 7-foot plaster Lincoln.

As I read French's words in letters to friends and family, along with stories told by his daughter and wife, the opening line of this book emerged: *Sometimes history shapes us.* I had to wonder, how did a boy who lived through the Civil War and the assassination of a beloved president make sense of the events he experienced? *And what we do can shape history.* I hope, through my words and Shawn Fields's beautifully rendered illustrations, readers can experience for themselves how that traumatic period in our country's history helped shape many of the epic works of public art Daniel created.

Many of Daniel's sculptures honor monumental Americans who reflected Lincoln's ideals, like his statues of James Oglethorpe (Savannah, Georgia), Thomas Starr King (San Francisco, California), and Wendell Phillips (Boston, Massachusetts), who, like Lincoln, opposed slavery. But it was the Lincoln Memorial itself that became Daniel's radiant expression of what it means for a person to become, over the years, very, very good at what he loves, and for that talent to remind and inspire a nation.

---

[14]Letter to Mrs. Albert Miller, November 30, 1913, Daniel Chester French Family Correspondence, Library of Congress.

Dan the Maker

"A sculptor is nine-tenths mechanic, and one-tenth poet."
—Daniel Chester French[15]

Daniel working on his Spirit of Life *sculpture on train tracks, Chesterwood 1914.*

Young Dan French was an early do-it-yourselfer. Today we might call him a *maker*, someone who invents in order to solve his or her needs. To become a world-famous artist, Daniel also used his skills as a mechanic, builder, inventor, designer, and collaborator.

On his family's farm, Dan was the one who plowed the straightest lines in the field and fixed the fences and the chicken coop. When he needed a new dresser, he built one himself. When he wanted to make a bust of his brother, he built a supporting armature from wood and wire. When it came time to enlarge his sculptures, he built his own pointing machine—an ingenious device invented in the eighteenth century to make copies of a clay or plaster model into stone.

Writing to his mentor, Thomas Ball, Dan included a drawing of his pointing machine, which he made almost entirely of brass. Dan confessed that though the machine worked, he may have been too experimental, like the cook who, when "following a new recipe for cake—left out the sugar & eggs for fear the result would be a failure and she should lose them. Her cake was always a failure. My machine would have been better had I put a few more dollars into it, but it works well as it is."[16]

Dan even built train tracks into the floor and out the door of his western Massachusetts studio so he could push sculptures out into the sunlight and rotate them. This helped him to see how a sculpture would look in daylight when installed in its public outdoor location. He experimented with innovative sculpting techniques throughout his life, once assembling a bronze statue of George Washington and his horse from many smaller pieces "like a giant jigsaw puzzle."

[15]"Old Berkshire Honored Again—Daniel French, the World Renowned Sculptor, Chooses to Make His Summer Home in the Village of Glendale," *Sunday Morning Call*, Pittsfield, MA, March 20, 1898.

[16]Letter to Thomas Ball, March 11, 1877, Daniel Chester French Family Correspondence, Library of Congress.

The Lincoln Memorial

The Lincoln Memorial dedication, May 30, 1922.

The Dedication

What would it have felt like to attend the dedication ceremony for the Lincoln Memorial? You might have felt a rush of excitement as 50,000 people poured onto the western end of the National Mall, just a ten-minute walk from the White House. If you were white and lucky enough to have a special printed ticket, you would have been ushered to a seat with a wooden back near the stage. You might have sat next to Civil War veterans from the North and South who had fought against each other in America's bloodiest conflict. Sitting together, they were a sign that the country was healing.

If you were black and were attending the ceremony to celebrate Lincoln, the great freer of slaves, even if you had a ticket, you would have been herded into a roped-off "colored section" by soldiers with guns and bayonets. There you would have sat on a bench with no back. According to Harold Holzer, author of the excellent biography *Monument Man: The Art and Life of Daniel Chester French*, "it was a stain on that day."

You would probably not have been surprised to hear that the lone African-American speaker, Robert Russa Moton, had been forced to rewrite his speech when the Lincoln Memorial Commission determined that his call for racial justice was too radical. After the ceremony, you might have stood gazing at the enormous statue and read Abraham Lincoln's Gettysburg Address,  which is carved in stone on the memorial's south wall. Lincoln's brief speech aspired to a "government of the people, by the people, for the people," no exceptions. Under the gaze of Daniel's inspiring statue, you might have walked out determined to make Lincoln's words a reality.

The Creators

In addition to Henry Bacon (the architect) and Daniel Chester French (the sculptor), three other artists contributed to this awe-inspiring memorial. Their names were Evelyn, Ernest, and Jules.

Evelyn Beatrice Longman created the decorative carvings inside the memorial. She was the first woman sculptor to be elected a full member of the National Academy of Design.

Ernest Barstow, an architectural sculptor, worked on the finer details of the memorial including the wreaths, eagles, and chains of flowers called festoons. He also carved the inscription behind Lincoln's head that is bathed in golden light at night. It reads:

IN THIS TEMPLE

AS IN THE HEARTS OF THE PEOPLE

FOR WHOM HE SAVED THE UNION

THE MEMORY OF ABRAHAM LINCOLN

IS ENSHRINED FOREVER

Barstow also carved Lincoln's Gettysburg Address on the south wall. On the north wall he carved Lincoln's Second Inaugural Address, which Lincoln delivered shortly before his death in 1865. It sought to welcome the South back into the Union "with malice towards none; charity for all."

Jules Guerin painted two canvas murals as a reminder of Lincoln's greatest achievements. In *Emancipation*, the Angel of Truth releases slaves. In *Unity*, the Angel of Truth brings together figures from the North and South. Each canvas is 60 feet long by 12 feet high and weighs 600 pounds.

And this roster of artists would not be complete if it did not include the Piccirilli brothers, artists in stone.

The Legacy

The Lincoln Memorial has been called "the great auditorium under the sky." It became a fitting stage for the Civil Rights movement.

When world-renowned African-American contralto Marian Anderson was refused an opportunity to sing at Constitution Hall in Washington, DC because she was black, Eleanor Roosevelt

The Piccirilli brothers piecing together Daniel's Abraham Lincoln statue in 1920 while Daniel looks on.

invited her to sing on the steps of the Lincoln Memorial instead. Seventeen years after the Lincoln Memorial dedication, on April 9, 1939, an audience of 75,000 fans, black and white, filled the mall to listen.

On August 28, 1963, Dr. Martin Luther King, Jr. delivered his "I Have a Dream" speech from the steps of the Lincoln Memorial to an audience of 250,000. Millions more watched on television. It became one of the most famous speeches in history and is memorialized by an inscribed marble slab on the spot where Dr. King stood that day.

The inauguration of Barack Obama as America's first black president on January 18, 2009, included a "We Are One" concert and celebration at the Lincoln Memorial that was attended by an estimated 400,000 people.

And yet the most powerful moments at the Lincoln Memorial are private ones. Standing on the marble floors, it is hard not to be inspired by the great president's mental and physical strength and his unshakable confidence in America, just as Daniel hoped.

Alone with a visionary president.

The Creations of Daniel Chester French

Daniel Chester French statues stand throughout the United States, including the following states and cities:

California: Glendale and San Francisco

Georgia: Atlanta (two statues) and Savannah

Illinois: Chicago (four statues)

Indiana: Muncie

Iowa: Council Bluffs

Kansas: Lawrence

Massachusetts: Boston (eleven), Cambridge (two), Concord (two), Milford, Milton, and Worcester (two)

Michigan: Detroit

Minnesota: Minneapolis and St. Paul (two)

Missouri: Kansas City and St. Louis (two)

Nebraska: Lincoln

New Hampshire: Concord (two), Exeter, and Franklin

New Jersey: Allamuchy

New York: Albany, Florida, Irvington, the Bronx (five), Brooklyn (six), Manhattan (five), and Saratoga Springs

Ohio: Cleveland (three)

Pennsylvania: Easton, Philadelphia (three), and Pittsburgh (two)

Rhode Island: Peace Dale

Wisconsin: Madison and Milwaukee

Washington, DC: (four)

You can also see Daniel's famous statue of George Washington on horseback in Paris, France, and a memorial tablet in Strasbourg, France.

Selected Resources

My research led me to many sources, including the French family papers at the Library of Congress and Williams College; Henry Flagg French's farm journals; newspapers published during Daniel's lifetime; books written by his wife, his daughter, and numerous scholars; and visits to the Concord Museum and to Chesterwood, Daniel's summer home and studio in Stockbridge, Massachusetts. Both Shawn Fields and I have been helped tremendously by generous librarians and museum curators.

Books

Craven, Wayne, *Sculpture in America* (University of Delaware Press, 1984)

Cresson, Margaret French, *Journey into Fame: The Life of Daniel Chester French* (Harvard University Press, 1947; reissued by Andesite Press, 2015)

French, Mary Adams, *Memories of a Sculptor's Wife* (Houghton Mifflin, 1928)

Goldstein, Ernest, *The Statue of Abraham Lincoln: A Masterpiece by Daniel Chester French* (Lerner Publications, 1997)

Gurney, George, *Sculpture in the Federal Triangle* (National Collection of Fine Arts, Smithsonian Institution Press, 1985)

Holzer, Harold, *Monument Man: The Life and Art of Daniel Chester French* (Princeton Architectural Press, 2019)

Miller, Natalie, *The Story of the Lincoln Memorial* (Children's Press, 1966)

Richman, Michael, *Daniel Chester French: An American Sculptor* (The Preservation Press, 1976)

Articles and Websites

National Park Service Lincoln Memorial website: www.nps.gov/linc/index.htm

Price, Willedene, "Daniel Chester French: The Artist as Historian," *Social Education*, Vol. 46, No.1 (January 1982)

Rettig, Polly M., "Daniel Chester French Home and Studio," *National Historic Landmark Documentation*, Washington, DC: US Department of the Interior, National Park Service, 1974 www.nps.gov/nr/twhp/wwwlps/lessons/100chesterwood/100facts3.htm

Places to Visit

Chesterwood. Daniel's summer home, studio, and gardens in Stockbridge, Massachusetts, is now a National Trust for Historic Preservation Site. Visitors of all ages marvel at the 7-foot plaster model for the Lincoln Memorial and many other finished works, maquettes, and working models. For more information, see www.chesterwood.org.

Concord Museum. This museum in Concord, Massachusetts, where Daniel became a sculptor, has a collection of French's work and is designing a new permanent exhibition dedicated to him. For more information, see www.concordmuseum.org.

Concord Free Public Library. The library offers access to Concord-related art, including work by Daniel Chester French. Among Daniel's work in the library's collection are an 1884 marble version of his 1879 bust from life of Ralph Waldo Emerson and the pair of owls he sculpted in 1871 (illustrated on page 23). For more information, see www.concordlibrary.org.

About the Quotes in This Book

On page 13, Dan's memory of Lincoln as "the man who saw straight when all the rest were seeing crooked" is from *Journey into Fame: The Life of Daniel Chester French,* by Margaret French Cresson (1947).

The words of the Concord Thinkers on page 15 are from the following sources:

Alcott, Amos Bronson, "Orphic Sayings." *The Dial,* Vol. I, No. 1, 85–98 (July 1840); Vol. I, No. 3, 351–361 (January 1841)

Alcott, Louisa May, *Little Women,* 1868 (reprinted by Penguin Books, 1953)

Emerson, Ralph Waldo, "Self-Reliance," 1841 (reprinted by Peter Pauper Press, 1967)

Fuller, Margaret, *Memoirs of Margaret Fuller Ossoli,* Vol. I, 1852, p. 132 (R. Bentley, London)

Hawthorne, Nathaniel, *Fanshawe,* 1828 (from Fredson Bowers, editor: *The Blithedale Romance and Fanshawe,* by Nathaniel Hawthorne; Ohio State University Press, 1965)

Thoreau, Henry David, *Walden; or, Life in the Woods,* 1854 (reprinted by J.M. Dent, London, 1908)

The quotes attributed to Dan's father and stepmother on page 20 are from *Journey into Fame: The Life of Daniel Chester French,* by Margaret French Cresson (1947).

Henry Bacon's quote in the caption on page 35 is from *The Story of the Lincoln Memorial,* by Natalie Miller (1966).

For two artsy women:
My mother Rosemarie Booth, who always loved to make
things beautiful, and Anne Brooke, who channeled her love of
art into preserving open spaces and historical buildings.
—LBS

AUTHOR'S ACKNOWLEDGMENTS

Taking an idea from clay to model to finished statue, a sculptor is helped by many hands. The same is true for a writer. I'm grateful to those who, over the last ten years, have helped make this book a reality.

Partners

Thank you, Carrie Hannigan, my agent, who saw the spark of a good story and who, expertly and with much-appreciated humor, guided it through to publication. Thank you, Shawn Fields, for your remarkable artistry and stellar thought partnership. Thank you, Kenzie Fields and the Fields family, for opening your home and art studio on my research venture to Western Massachusetts.

Readers

Thank you, Gale Pryor, Jackie Davies, Candace Fleming, Anne Hayden, and my invaluable writing groups (Walden Writers Group and Children's Nonfiction Writers), for your many thoughtful critiques along the way.

Daniel Chester French scholars

Thank you, Harold Holzer, for your inspiring scholarship and for generously responding to a flurry of emails in the final months of writing. Thank you, Michael Richman, author of a dissertation on French, for your early clarifications and encouragement.

Librarians and curators

I am grateful to Dana Pilson, curatorial researcher at Chesterwood, and Donna Hassler, Chesterwood's executive director, for their many thoughtful and upbeat responses to inquiries; to Wayne G. Hammond, head librarian of the Chapin Library at Williams College (custodian of the Chesterwood Archives), for helping me track down a seemingly endless number of French family correspondences and for helping the publisher with photo research; to Thayer Tolles, curator at the Metropolitan Museum of Art, and Dan Preston, editor of the Papers of James Monroe at the University of Mary Washington, for their timely and expert responses; to Leslie Perrin Wilson (special collections curator), Karen Ahearn (head children's librarian), and Fayth Chamberland (children's librarian) at the Concord Free Public Library; and to Tom Putnam (*executive director*), Carol Haines (manager of exhibition and designs), and David Wood (curator) at the Concord Museum for sharing their expertise and passion for children's books and Concord history.

Funders

I am indebted to dear Jonathan Keyes and the Concord Circle—Peter Brooke, Russell and Lee Robb, and Pierce and Elise Browne—for their enthusiastic support and generosity in helping to underwrite this book, and to the Concord Museum for providing the vehicle for that support.

Publisher

Thank you to Jon Eaton and the team at Tilbury House Publishers for being the glue that pulled together the many pieces of this wonderful book.

Supporters

And last but not least, I am grateful to my home team—Anna, Ted, Jack, John, and my sister Cynthia Hamburger—who encouraged me every step of the way, pulled me out of the weeds when necessary, and never doubted that I would finish this book. —LBS

ILLUSTRATOR'S NOTE

I illustrated this book mostly using ink pens. Before applying ink, I usually draw a picture in pencil, which I like because it is easy to erase. Once the pencil drawing looks good to me, I lightly trace it onto another sheet of paper and apply ink over the tracing. When I erase any leftover pencil lines, all that is left is the finished pen drawing. Daniel Chester French worked in a similar way, sculpting what are called "sketch models" in clay, which allowed for many adjustments before making his finished sculptures in marble.

As noted in the timeline in the back of this book, Dan's mother passed away when he was six, and his father remarried soon after. Dan's stepmother was energetic and was very supportive of Dan's interest in sculpture. She encouraged his father to take notice of Dan's talent. I too grew up with an energetic and very supportive stepmother in addition to a wonderful mother and father. Now that I am married, I also have the support of my wife's stepmother and father. I think that if we look around, we can each notice people who are supporting us and our dreams, and feel grateful. —SF

Photo Credits

Page 53, bird sketch, Chapin Library, Williams College, Chesterwood Archives; **p.54**, *Matchmaking* statuette, Concord Museum, Wikimedia Commons; **p.54**, *The Minuteman,* National Park Service; **p.55**, *The Republic*, C. D. Arnold photo courtesy The Art Institute of Chicago, Ryerson & Burnham archives; **p.55**, Chesterwood studio, Library of Congress; **p.56**, French in 1915, Chapin Library, Williams College, Chesterwood Archives; **p.56**, French and Bacon at the Lincoln Memorial, Library of Congress; **p.57**, French at Chesterwood with George Washington statue, Chapin Library, Williams College, Chesterwood Archives; **p.57**, French at Chesterwood with seated Lincoln, Chapin Library, Williams College, Chesterwood Archives; **p.58**, French at Chesterwood, Chapin Library, Williams College, Chesterwood Archives; **p.59**, Lincoln Memorial dedication, Harris & Ewing glass-plate photo, Library of Congress; **p.59**, Lincoln's face, Zason Smith photo, iStock; **p.60**, photographer unknown, National Archives and Records Administration, Washington, DC, copy print from Chapin Library, Williams College, Chesterwood Archives; **p.61**, Library of Congress; **p.63**, Library of Congress.

Text © 2019 by Linda Booth Sweeney • Illustrations © 2019 by Shawn Fields
Hardcover ISBN 978-0-88448-643-5 • eBook ISBN 978-0-88448-645-9

Library of Congress Control Number: 2019939492

Book design by Frame25 Productions
Printed in China through Four Colour Print Group

18 19 20 XXX 10 9 8 7 6 5 4 3 2

CONCORD MUSEUM

Monument Maker is published in association with the Concord Museum.

Tilbury House Publishers
12 Starr Street
Thomaston, Maine 04861
www.tilburyhouse.com

Concord Museum
200 Lexington Rd
Concord, MA 01742
www.concordmuseum.org